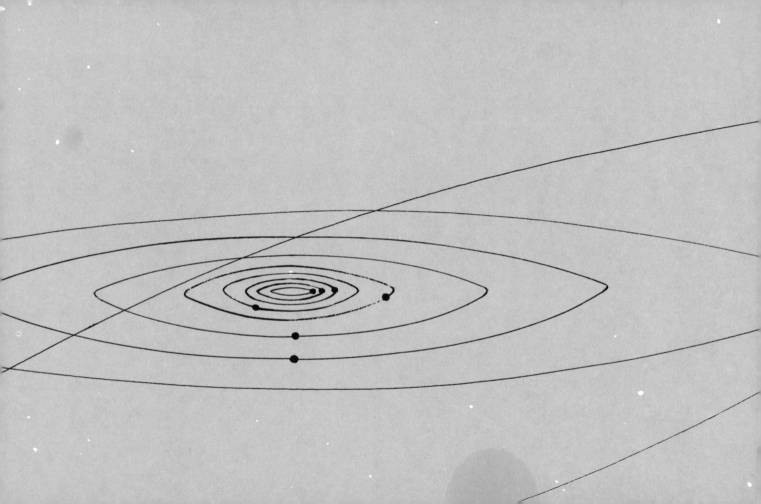

I CAN READ ABOUT

PLANETS

Written by Darrow Schecter

Illustrated by Joel Snyder

Troll Associates

The word *planet* means wanderer.
The Ancient Greeks called the planets wanderers
because the planets would always change
their positions in the sky.

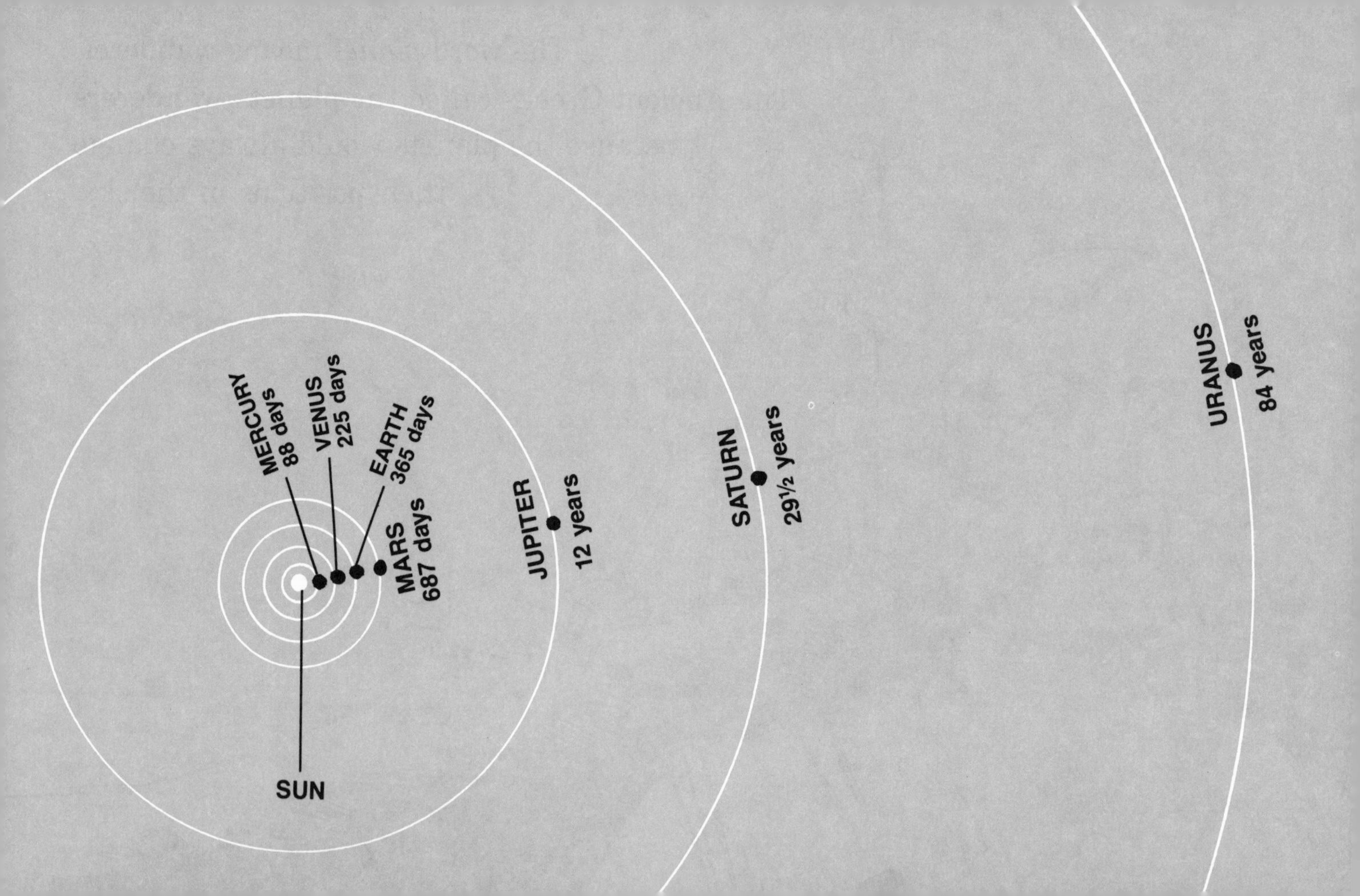

MERCURY
88 days

VENUS
225 days

EARTH
365 days

MARS
687 days

SUN

JUPITER
12 years

SATURN
29½ years

URANUS
84 years

NEPTUNE
165 years

PLUTO
248 years

Today we know that each planet moves around the sun. The journey that each planet makes around the sun is called an *orbit*.

Each planet is found at a different distance from the sun. This is why it takes each planet a different amount of time to orbit the sun.

moon

What exactly is a planet? Planets are sometimes called heavenly bodies. This means that they are found in space. Scientists who study the planets and other things in space are called astronomers. They study the planets with high-powered telescopes, computers, and space satellites. They often do their work in an observatory.

Astronomers have discovered many things about the planets and stars. All stars are really suns. Some stars are very much like our own sun. Our sun is much larger than any of the planets.

Stars give off their own light. But planets do not give off their own light. They are like mirrors. They reflect light the way our moon reflects light from the sun.

The planets *seem* to move very fast. But this is only because the planets are closer to us than stars. Stars are much, much farther away.

All planets orbit the sun. Some planets have smaller bodies that also orbit around them. These bodies are called moons or natural satellites.

Moons and satellites travel close to the planet they are orbiting. Their journey around the planet is always a shorter trip than the planet's journey around the sun.

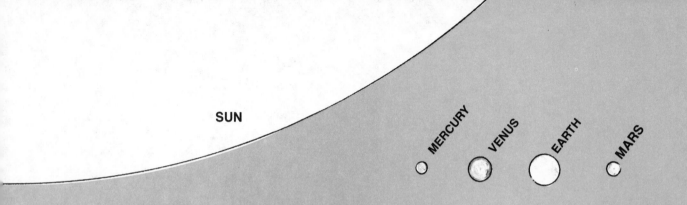

The nine planets that orbit the sun, and
the sun itself, make up most of our solar system.

The first four planets from the sun are called the inner planets.

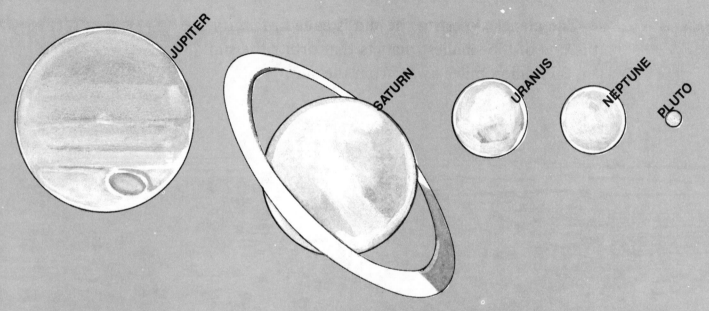

The last five are called the outer planets.

The planet closest to the sun is called Mercury.
It is one of the smallest planets that orbits the sun.
It is 36 million miles away from the sun.

There are things about Mercury you would probably like and things you would not like. It takes Mercury only 88 days to orbit the sun. This means that a year on Mercury is only 88 days. If you lived on Mercury, your birthday would come four times as often as on Earth.

But since this planet is so close to the sun, Mercury may become as hot as 800 degrees on its surface. You might not like that.

As it moves farther away from the sun, each planet takes longer to orbit the sun than the one before it.

The planet after Mercury is Venus. Venus is like the Earth in many ways. Astronomers call Venus the twin sister of Earth.

A year on Venus is 225 days long. It takes Venus longer to go around the sun than it takes Mercury. Venus is famous because it is brighter than any of the other planets. Only the sun and the moon are brighter than Venus.

You should know all about the third planet from the sun, because you live on it. Earth is the third planet from the sun. It is 93 million miles away from the sun. It has a natural satellite — the moon.

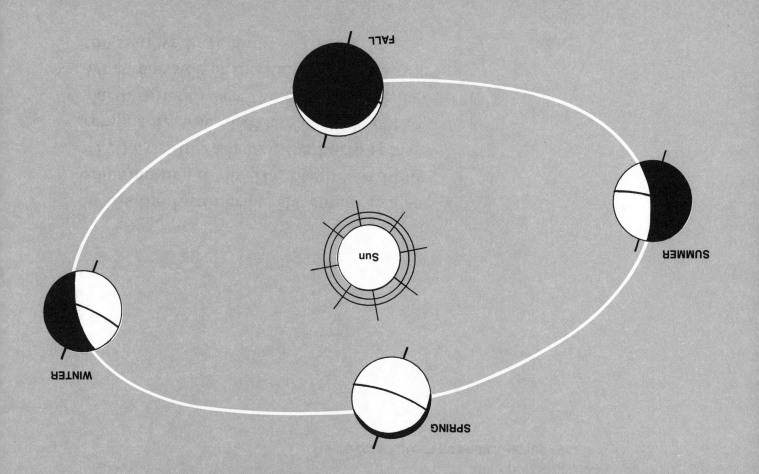

As the Earth orbits the sun, it is also spinning like a top. The Earth is *rotating on its axis. In 24 hours,* the Earth spins completely around. When our side of the Earth turns toward the sun, we have day. When our side of the Earth turns away from the sun, we have night.

149 600 000 KILOMETERS FROM THE SUN

Another thing about *your* planet is that as it orbits the sun, it tilts. During its 365-day trip around the sun, the Earth gets different amounts of sunlight. This causes the seasons.

Why does it get cold in winter? During the winter, our part of the Earth is tilted away from the sun and gets less of the sun's rays. During the summer, our part of the Earth is tilted toward the sun and gets more direct sunlight.

This tilting of the Earth also causes the in-between seasons of spring and fall. It helps the flowers to blossom in spring, and the leaves to fall in autumn. Winter, spring, summer and fall: Our tilting Earth travels around the sun in a year's journey.

The fourth planet from the sun is Mars.
The planet Mars is named after the Roman god of war because
of its red color. Mars has seasons because it tilts toward
the sun the way Earth tilts toward the sun.
    Spacecraft have studied the soil of Mars and have sent
back photographs of the surface of Mars.

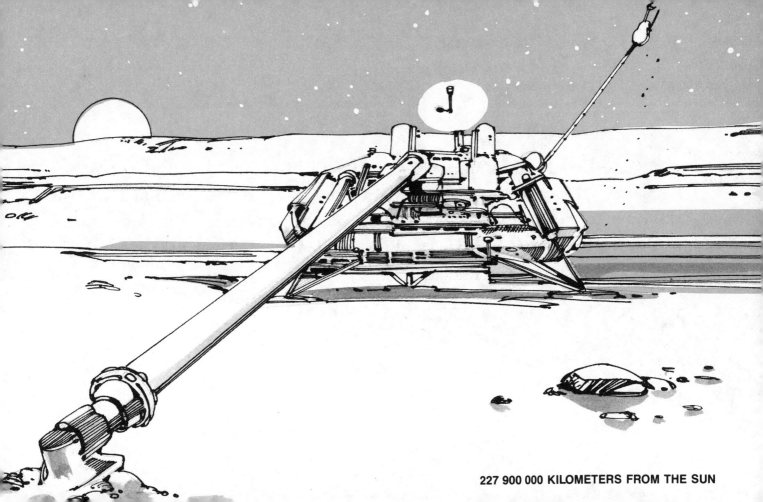

227 900 000 KILOMETERS FROM THE SUN

It takes Mars 687 days to orbit the sun.
Every 15 to 17 years, Mars comes very close to the Earth and sun.
This is a good time for Earth to study Mars.

There are two satellites around Mars. Their names are
Deimos and Phobos.

Sun

The fifth planet from the sun is the largest of all known planets. It is Jupiter. This planet is eleven times larger in diameter than Earth. Jupiter is one of the brightest planets. It has bands of different colors across it. Jupiter also has a large reddish spot.

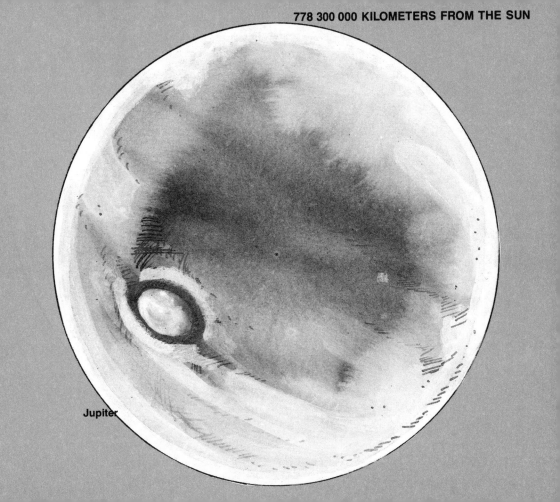

Earth

Jupiter

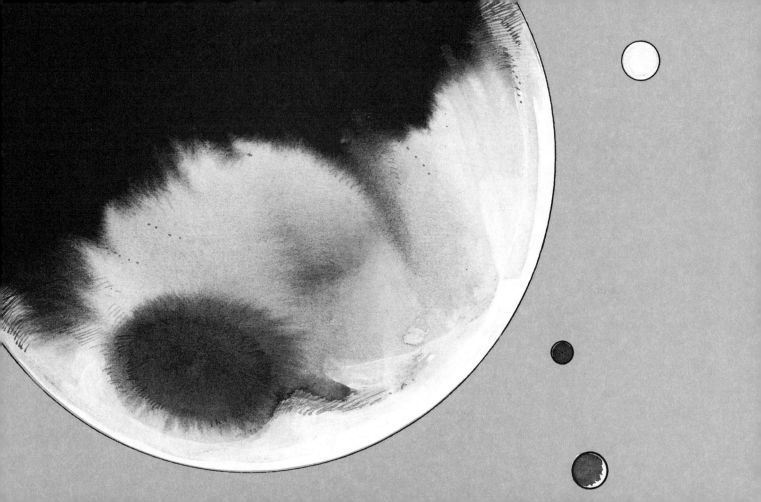

Jupiter is puzzling to astronomers because it is hidden. Its actual surface cannot be seen through a telescope. It is hidden by clouds of swirling gases.

Jupiter is 480 million miles from the sun. If you're on Jupiter, you'll have to wait 12 years to orbit the sun...Maybe you'd rather get off at one of Jupiter's 16 moons instead.

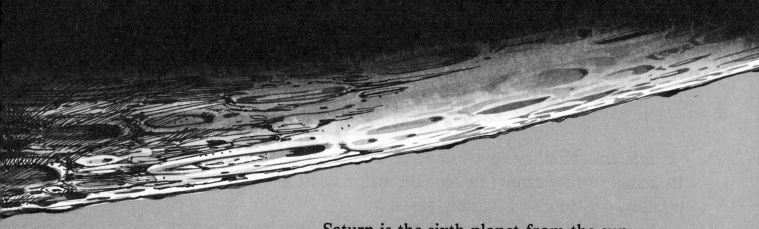

Saturn is the sixth planet from the sun.
It is the second largest planet. Only Jupiter is
larger.

Saturn is famous for its rings. At one time
astronomers thought that there was only
one ring. Later they discovered that there
were a number of icy rings around Saturn.

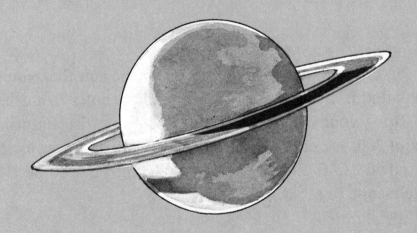

1 427 000 000 KILOMETERS FROM THE SUN

Saturn is the farthest planet from the sun that you can see without a telescope. It is 900 million miles from the sun.

Bring your warmest clothes if you ever visit Saturn. It is about 300 degrees below zero there. Saturn has at least 23 satellites. The largest is named Titan, but you need a telescope to see it.

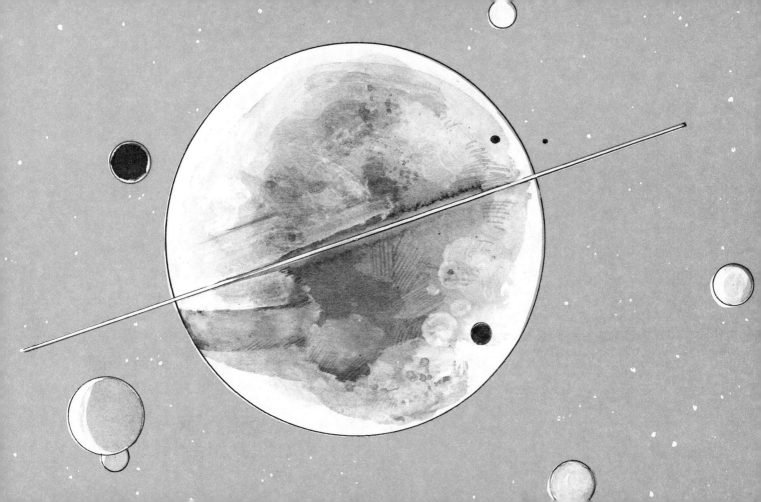

The last three planets are very far from the sun.
They are so far away that no one can be exactly sure what
they are really like.

There is still much to learn about them.

The seventh planet from the sun is called Uranus.
When viewing Uranus through a telescope, astronomers
can see a faint green glow. Uranus has five moons
and at least nine rings around it. Since Uranus is
so far away, it takes this planet 84 years to orbit
the sun.

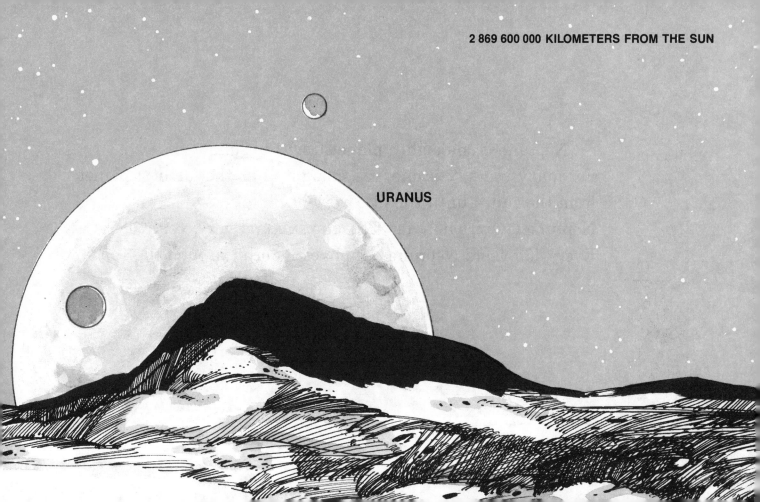

URANUS

Neptune is the eighth planet from the sun.
For many years Neptune was thought to be the farthest planet
from the sun — until the discovery of Pluto!
Neptune is extremely far from the sun and very, very cold.
Every 165 years Neptune completes its orbit around the sun.

Neptune

4 496 600 000 KILOMETERS FROM THE SUN

And finally there is the ninth planet, Pluto.
Pluto is the farthest planet from the sun that we know of.
It is more than 3½ billion miles from the sun.

It is a tiny planet. It is so small that some astronomers believe that Pluto is not a planet, but a moon that broke off from Neptune. Pluto is so very far away that it is still a mysterious planet.

5 900 000 000 KILOMETERS FROM THE SUN

Now you know about the nine planets and the sun
that make up our solar system. But sometime in the future
a new planet may be discovered, or an old one may disappear.

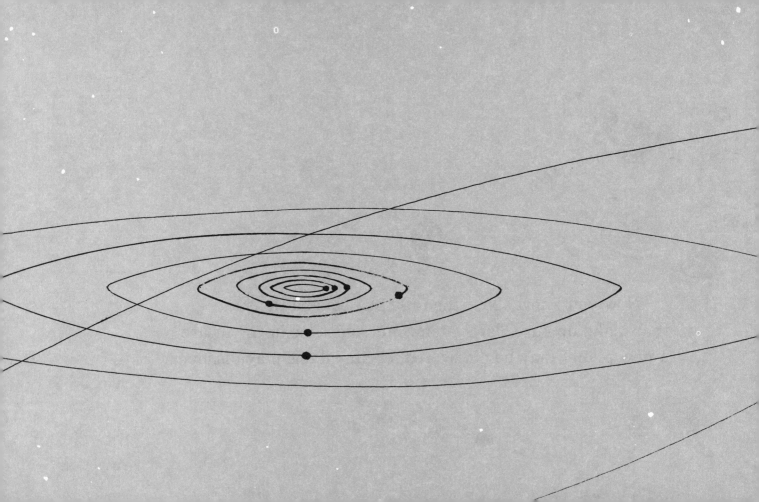

New discoveries are always being made.
We cannot be certain about what lies beyond our solar system.
But our solar system is part of the universe. And the universe
is a never-ending wonder that has puzzled and amazed people
since the beginning of time.

And, in time to come,
we will learn more about
the mysteries of outer space.